LION VS. CAPE BUFFALO

BY KIERAN DOWNS

BELLWETHER MEDIA · MINNEAPOLIS, MN

T0020128

Torque brims with excitement
perfect for thrill-seekers of all kinds.
Discover daring survival skills, explore
uncharted worlds, and marvel at mighty
engines and extreme sports. In *Torque* books,
anything can happen. Are you ready?

This edition first published in 2021 by Bellwether Media, Inc.

No part of this publication may be reproduced in whole or in part without written
permission of the publisher. For information regarding permission, write to
Bellwether Media, Inc., Attention: Permissions Department,
6012 Blue Circle Drive, Minnetonka, MN 55343.

Library of Congress Cataloging-in-Publication Data

Names: Downs, Kieran, author.
Title: Lion vs. cape buffalo / by Kieran Downs.
Other titles: Lion versus cape buffalo
Description: Minneapolis, MN : Bellwether Media, 2021. | Series: Torque:
   animal battles | Includes bibliographical references and index. |
   Audience: Ages 7-12 | Audience: Grades 4-6 | Summary: "Amazing
   photography accompanies engaging information about the fighting
   abilities of lions and Cape buffalo. The combination of high-interest
   subject matter and light text is intended for students in grades 3
   through 7"– Provided by publisher.
Identifiers: LCCN 2020041139 (print) | LCCN 2020041140 (ebook) | ISBN
   9781644874608 (library binding) | ISBN 9781648342530 (paperback) | ISBN
   9781648341373 (ebook)
Subjects: LCSH: Lion–Juvenile literature. | African buffalo–Juvenile literature.
Classification: LCC QL737.C23 D5855 2021 (print) | LCC QL737.C23 (ebook)
   | DDC 599.757–dc23
LC record available at https://lccn.loc.gov/2020041139
LC ebook record available at https://lccn.loc.gov/2020041140

Text copyright © 2021 by Bellwether Media, Inc. TORQUE and associated logos
are trademarks and/or registered trademarks of Bellwether Media, Inc.

Editor: Christina Leaf   Designer: Josh Brink

Printed in the United States of America, North Mankato, MN.

TABLE OF CONTENTS

THE COMPETITORS

Many animals roam the African **savanna**. But one **predator** rules them all. Lions are known as the king of beasts. These large cats take their choice of **prey**.

But not all prey goes down without a fight. Cape buffalo are more than able to **defend** themselves. Could they defeat the king of beasts?

AFRICAN LION PROFILE

| 0 | 5 FEET | 10 FEET |

LENGTH
UP TO 7 FEET
(2.1 METERS)

WEIGHT
UP TO 500 POUNDS
(227 KILOGRAMS)

HABITAT

SCRUBLANDS   SAVANNAS   WOODLANDS

AFRICAN LION RANGE

RANGE

Lions are the second-biggest cats in the world. They can weigh up to 500 pounds (227 kilograms). These big cats have golden-brown fur. It lets them hide from prey in their grassy homes.

Lions live in groups called prides. They work together to hunt for food. These **carnivores** will eat whatever meat they can find.

PRIDE

MAKING NOISE

A lion's roar can be heard from up to 5 miles (8 kilometers) away!

Cape buffalo are considered pests to farmers. The buffalo break fences, eat crops, and spread diseases to farm cows.

Cape buffalo are built to be tough. These large, dark-colored **mammals** can weigh more than 1,800 pounds (816 kilograms). They have wide horns that meet in the middle of their heads.

Cape buffalo live in large herds. Some herds can have up to 2,000 buffalo! They are found near water in many different **habitats**

CAPE BUFFALO PROFILE

WEIGHT
OVER 1,800 POUNDS
(816 KILOGRAMS)

6 FEET

4 FEET

HEIGHT
AROUND 5 FEET
(1.5 METERS)
AT THE SHOULDER

2 FEET

HABITAT

PLAINS   RAIN FORESTS   SAVANNAS   SWAMPS

CAPE BUFFALO RANGE

■ RANGE

SECRET WEAPONS

Lions have several weapons to take down prey. Their teeth can do a lot of harm. A lion's **canine teeth** can be up to 3.9 inches (10 centimeters) long!

Cape buffalo are huge. But that does not slow them down. They charge at speeds of up to 37 miles (60 kilometers) per hour! They run at enemies headfirst.

CAPE BUFFALO TOP SPEED

37 MILES (60 KILOMETERS) PER HOUR

CAPE BUFFALO

28 MILES (45 KILOMETERS) PER HOUR

HUMAN

1 INCH

0

LION CLAW
2.5 CENTIMETERS

Lions also have sharp, curved claws. These can be more than 1 inch (2.5 centimeters) long. They use their claws to hold on to enemies during attacks.

SECRET WEAPONS

SPEED

POINTED HORNS

LARGE HERDS

BOSSING AROUND

The area where a male Cape buffalo's horns come together is called a boss.

Cape buffalo's horns can reach more than 4 feet (1.2 meters) wide. They come together to form a hard helmet on male buffalo's heads. Their pointed ends can do a lot of damage!

SHARP TEETH **SHARP CLAWS** **LARGE PRIDES**

Prides work together to hunt larger prey. They attack from all sides. Many bites weaken their enemy faster. They make quick work of prey!

Cape buffalo herds help keep each other safe from predators. The large number of buffalo scares away most predators. Cape buffalo **communicate** if danger does come close. They warn the herd.

FEATHERED FRIENDS

Oxpeckers are birds that eat bugs off of the backs of Cape buffalo. They also warn the buffalo of danger by hissing if they see a lion!

ATTACK MOVES

Lions are smart hunters. Prides stay hidden. They circle around their prey. Then, one lion will scare the prey into the waiting group. The prey has no escape!

Cape buffalo can be **aggressive**.
They are not afraid to go on the attack.
The buffalo will often chase possible enemies,
even if they have not been attacked.

Lions pounce on their enemies to take them down. They hold on tight with sharp claws. A bite to the neck finishes off the prey.

LUNCH LINE

Male lions are often the first to eat. Female lions eat next. Cubs eat last.

If a Cape buffalo herd feels danger, it may **stampede**. Many buffalo will all start running the same way. Anything stuck in the path of the herd is crushed!

READY, FIGHT!

A lion spots a Cape buffalo feeding. It pounces on the buffalo's back. The buffalo tries to run. But the lion holds on. It bites at the buffalo's neck.

The wounded buffalo shakes off the lion. Now it is angry! The buffalo charges. It downs the lion with its horns. This buffalo will not be a meal today!

GLOSSARY

aggressive—ready to fight

canine teeth—long, pointed teeth that are often the sharpest in the mouth

carnivores—animals that only eat meat

communicate—to share thoughts and feelings using sounds, faces, and actions

defend—to protect

habitats—the homes or areas where animals prefer to live

mammals—warm-blooded animals that have backbones and feed their young milk

predator—an animal that hunts other animals for food

prey—animals that are hunted by other animals for food

savanna—a flat grassland in Africa with very few trees

stampede—to run in a panic, often in a large group

TO LEARN MORE

AT THE LIBRARY

Schuetz, Kari. *Cape Buffalo and Oxpeckers*. Minneapolis, Minn.: Bellwether Media, 2019.

Sommer, Nathan. *Lion vs. Hyena Clan*. Minneapolis, Minn.: Bellwether Media, 2020.

Wilsdon, Christina. *Ultimate Predatorpedia: The Most Complete Predator Reference Ever*. Washington, D.C.: National Geographic Kids, 2018.

ON THE WEB

FACTSURFER

Factsurfer.com gives you a safe, fun way to find more information.

1. Go to www.factsurfer.com

2. Enter "lion vs. Cape buffalo" into the search box and click 🔍.

3. Select your book cover to see a list of related content.

INDEX